THE LITANY OF THE ELVES

T0364281

THE LITANY OF THE ELVES

BY

J. C. LAWSON, M.A.

FELLOW AND TUTOR OF PEMBROKE COLLEGE, CAMBRIDGE
TEMPORARY ACTING LIEUTENANT-COMMANDER R.N.V.R.
AND COMMANDER, BRITISH NAVAL MISSION TO GREECE

CAMBRIDGE
AT THE UNIVERSITY PRESS
1919

CAMBRIDGE
UNIVERSITY PRESS

University Printing House, Cambridge CB2 8BS, United Kingdom

Published in the United States of America by Cambridge University Press, New York

Cambridge University Press is part of the University of Cambridge.

It furthers the University's mission by disseminating knowledge in the pursuit of education, learning and research at the highest international levels of excellence.

www.cambridge.org
Information on this title: www.cambridge.org/9781107683976

© Cambridge University Press 1919

First published 1919
First paperback edition 2013

A catalogue record for this publication is available from the British Library

ISBN 978-1-107-68397-6 Paperback

DEDICATED TO
ROBIN, ROSEM'RY, MICHAEL, AND DAVID,
THE CHILDREN OF MY BROTHER
HARRY SACKVILLE LAWSON
LATE HEADMASTER OF BUXTON COLLEGE
AND TEMPORARY LIEUTENANT R.G.A.
WHO FELL IN FRANCE
FEBRUARY 5, 1918

The Litany of the Elves

T was early morning when I woke. My window looked out, over olive-trees and pepper-trees on the slope of Lycabettus, across the dusty brown plain below just dappled here and there with green after the autumn rains; and beyond was the great misty grey mound of Hymettus over which the sun had not yet climbed, though the sky above was flushed and rosy. So it wasn't the sun that woke me. It was a faint, faint chorus of silvery voices singing to the music of far-off bells, so faint that the waking world, it seemed, lay still a while longer to listen. I must have been listening to it too in my sleep without knowing, because when I woke it didn't surprise me at all. I knew quite well of course that it couldn't be the Greek soldiers down in the barracks by the dusty plain, nor the monks in the little white monastery with its tall black cypresses just beyond the garden wall. The monks and the soldiers do often sing early in the morning, but their singing is a funny whiny noise made through their noses. And really I knew who

was singing without having to think; it is only the elves who can sing quite like that.

I wonder if you know about the elves. When God made the angels, He didn't want to have only grown-up people in heaven; so He made elves too, a sort of angel-children. Angels don't get any older, you see; they've had lots and lots of birthdays, but grown-up angels don't get old or tired, and the elves are children always and don't grow up. They are good children of course, just as good as the big angels; only as they are such little people, they have to help God in ways suited to little people. God gives them the flowers to look after, the wild flowers chiefly in the fields and woods, because men and women look after garden-flowers for themselves, and, if the elves do put any wild flowers among them, the gardener calls them weeds and pulls them up, or pushes a noisy mowing-machine up and down the lawn and chops all the daisies' heads off. So elves don't often come into gardens. The one where I heard them singing had wild patches left, so perhaps that was why they came there. And long, long ago too they used to be very fond of Athens; there is a hill still called after them —"the Hill of the Nymphs"—because what we call elves the old Greeks used to call nymphs.

The elves look after the wild animals too and the birds and butterflies and bees, in fact everything that runs or flies about, lizards. and toads and tortoises along with the rest. Not that some of them want much looking after; toads have very few troubles, and tortoises don't care much about being amused; they never feel frolicsome, and generally draw back into their shell if the elves make any advances to them, though they are quite grateful if they are shown where there are dandelions to eat. But I needn't tell you yet how the elves look after animals, because there is something about that in the song they were singing.

So first I'll give you the song I heard that morning, and then I'll tell you what I think it was all about. I remembered some of the words of it the moment I woke up, because as I told you I must have been listening to the song in my sleep. When I woke I could still hear the music, but it was harder to catch all the words; still afterwards by degrees as I tried to write the song down, the verses I had heard in my sleep seemed to come back to me. I think they are all there, because they come exactly to twelve, and it is very likely that angels and elves should count in twelves; there were twelve Apostles and twelve of other things in the Bible; and country folk too, who are likely to know more about elves and to have learnt more from them in old times than people who live in towns, still count their eggs and apples, and out here their oranges and pomegranates, in dozens.

The tune, I'm sure, as well as the words, must have

been made up by the elves themselves. It seems they must have taken bits out of two other tunes they like, and fitted them together. Do you know the tune of "Robin Adair"? Well, the beginning and the end are like that, only changed a little so as to go slower and more like a litany, and in the middle there are some lines taken from one of the tunes to which we sing "Nearer, my God, to Thee." And the music that goes with it is like the faint chiming of church-bells a long, long way off. The heather comes out again here in the autumn on Hymettus, so perhaps it was millions of little heather-bells ringing that I heard; but I can't tell you whether it was the elves who rang them, or if they asked the bees there to stop making honey for a little and ring the bells for them while they sang. Their song isn't at all hard to learn if you like to sing it yourselves. It is called "the Litany of the Elves."

Air by the Elves   *Music of the Bells by Gra*

or

Ripples in

clime, Give peace, dear   God,   Ripples in   fai - - ry chime, Give peace, dear
8va

God. From East and West we've come,   To   wel - come   Mi - - - chael

home,   Grant   he   no   more   need roam; Give peace, dear
8va

God.
8va

rall e dim

5

The Litany of the Elves.

One prayer from every clime,
"Give peace, dear God,"
Ripples in fairy chime,
"Give peace, dear God,"
From East and West we've come
To welcome Michael home;
Grant he no more need roam,
Give peace, dear God.

One prayer, not for ourselves,
"Give peace, dear God,"
From all Thy faithful elves,
"Give peace, dear God,"
Chimes over hill and dell,
Chimes o'er the ocean-swell,
Chimes wheresoe'er we dwell;
Give peace, dear God.

Only big angels see—
Give peace, dear God,
Why such sad things must be—
Give peace, dear God,
Death strown o'er field and flood,
Tears of lone womanhood,
Children who cry for food,—
Give peace, dear God.

Vain must be Hell's whole might—
Give peace, dear God,
Where true men front the fight—
Give peace, dear God,
Strengthened by Michael's arm,
Restored by Raphael's balm,
Soothed by sweet Gabriel's calm;
Give peace, dear God.

Yet passes day by day,
Give peace, dear God,
No angels join our play,
Give peace, dear God,
"Fight on," cries Michael, "yet,"
Shrewd Raphael's lips are set,
And Gabriel's cheeks are wet;
Give peace, dear God.

The guardian-angels too—
Give peace, dear God,
Veil their sad eyes from view—
Give peace, dear God,
Rememb'ring some lone grave
Where lies smiling and brave
One whom they hoped to save;
Give peace, dear God.

We frailer elfin-folk,—
Give peace, dear God,
Frail as sweet-briar to oak,—
Give peace, dear God,
Serve not in men's behoof:
We, shunning road and roof,
Work in the wilds aloof;
Give peace, dear God.

Ours is to soothe the pain—
Give peace, dear God,
Of flower athirst for rain—
Give peace, dear God,
Or bird with crippled wing
And each wee furry thing
That has a bruise to bring;
Give peace, dear God.

7

Thorn picked from quivering paw,—
Give peace, dear God,
Herbs for sick swollen maw,—
Give peace, dear God,
Lost hoards of nuts re-found,
Storm-beaten nests made sound,
These fill our little round;
Give peace, dear God.

But we've a fine surprise,—
Give peace, dear God,
Michael will rub his eyes—
Give peace, dear God,
Mazed at weak elfin-hood,
Wardens of mead and wood,
Working for human good;
Give peace, dear God.

We now help men as well,—
Give peace, dear God,
Brave men who fought and fell,—
Give peace, dear God,
Planting a pansy-plot
Rimmed with forget-me-not,
Over each hallowed spot;
Give peace, dear God.

Weaving from gossamer—
Give peace, dear God,
Suits for their souls to wear,—
Give peace, dear God,
Embroid'ring kerchiefs gay
For God to wipe away
Tears from all eyes one day;
Give peace, dear God.

8

I couldn't help wondering why the elves were singing about Michael's home-coming and the welcome they would all give him,—why, I mean, they were doing it that particular morning. It was the third of November, and Michael's birthday when all angels and elves who can be spared from duty have a holiday is the twenty-ninth of September. But then Michael, you see, has been so busy these last four years that he may not have been able to go home for his birthday, and the holiday may have been put off. There have been so many fronts where his help was wanted, on the Marne and the Somme, the Strymon and Jordan and Euphrates, and naturally he couldn't leave all his soldier-angels to go on fighting while he took a holiday, not even though he knew how disappointed the elves would be if his leave was put off again.

But perhaps when All Saints' Day came and All Souls' Day—they are the first two days of November, you know,—he thought that as the fighting was over on some of the fronts he could be spared for a little, and it would be a chance not only of giving the elves the holiday which they had missed on his birthday, but of meeting again many old comrades whom he had led and cheered on in all those battles. So the elves who had made up their litany to sing on Michael's birthday, kept it till All Saints' and All Souls' Days, for which it was just as good, and sang it for the first time then.

And perhaps when Michael heard it, he asked the elves to sing it every morning,—when they were back at work, just the same,—until the war ended and peace came, because by singing a pretty prayer like that they would be helping the men and angels who were fighting, as well as all the women and children who were suffering at home. And so November the third was the first morning that they were singing it in the fields and woods when they came back to their work there.

Michael seems to be the elves' favourite among their big brothers. When he isn't away fighting, he often shows them his big sword, which they can hardly lift, and his armour. His sword is polished so bright that it looks as if it were on fire, and the jewels of the hilt keep twinkling in its light, twinkling like the elves' own eyes. And his armour is lovely too, lots and lots of little steel scales with curly ribbons of gold inlaid in them, and so cunningly jointed together that it fits quite close to him and feels just as soft and comfy as if it were made of wool. And sometimes the elves pretend that Michael's armour isn't quite clean, and take turns to rub the scales bright, though really they are so bright all the time that the elves can see their own faces in them.

And then too Michael plays games with them when there is no war to keep him away. Hide-and-seek is their favourite, because among the trees in the woods where they play it is no advantage to Michael that he is so big and strong. He is like a falcon playing hide-and-seek with swallows or with dragon-flies, and the elves dart about from one hiding-place to another just as quickly as he can. And then they are so small that they can hide in a clump of ferns quite easily, and Michael is so big that he has to find a very thick tree-trunk; and it makes the elves very merry if the tips of Michael's wings are just showing from behind the tree, and it is all they can do not to laugh out loud before they have pounced upon him. So they have a lot of fun, and the elves very often win.

Of course it isn't Michael only who plays with them. Raphael and Gabriel and all the angels love having games with them. And though Michael may be their favourite big brother, they are very fond of Raphael and Gabriel and all the others too. Raphael is the doctor-angel, and knows all about sick or wounded animals as well as men. So he can tell the elves what herbs and plants make good medicine for all the wild creatures. When the baby bunnies eat too much wet grass and get little swollen tummies, the elves tell them to nibble a little dry sage or parsley and then go to bed in their burrows. And for scratches and cuts and bites there is a plant called balsam with a juice which takes the pain away and makes them better. And the elves always know too where there are dock-leaves growing, and if one of their pets—

because all the animals are their pets—tries to play with wasps and gets his nose stung, they show him where to cool it against the big fresh leaves. And if they don't quite know what is the matter, they tuck them up in their holes or nests and tell them to keep warm, just like our doctors do, and very often they are better in the morning.

And then Gabriel too: the elves are very very fond of Gabriel. He knows best of all the angels how to comfort them when their pets die, and he has such a sweet gentle face and is so kind to anyone in trouble. He is just like a mother to them. And I shouldn't be surprised if it was Gabriel they told first when they thought of making up their litany to sing on Michael's birthday, and made him promise not to tell any of the other angels, because it was a secret. And perhaps he even helped them a little in making it up, and heard them sing it each day in some quiet spot until they all knew it right through. I'm sure he must have liked that line about peace which keeps on coming in every verse, because he is the angel of peace and would love to hear all the elves praying God to give peace.

Perhaps you are wondering why the elves say nothing about Uriel, the other archangel, in their song. That does seem rather funny. But then Uriel is so busy in his office that the elves don't often see him. You see they live out in the woods and fields and don't often go near houses; they may just peep into some country cottage now and then, where there is some child left all alone at home or where a cat they have met in the woods is basking quietly by the fire; but you wouldn't expect them to go into an office. Besides Uriel has nothing to amuse them with there; he would much sooner come out and play with them, when he can, in the country; only he has been so busy lately, just as busy as Michael, and the things that he does his work with wouldn't interest the elves like Michael's bright sword and armour. Uriel just has a huge great book in which he is always writing; and there isn't anything much to see,—just a name at the top of each page, and three long columns ruled down it headed "Thoughts," "Words," and "Deeds," and in each column he has to enter notes with good or bad marks for the good or bad things which people think and say and do.

A lot of the things he has to write down are beautiful and he loves them, and others are very ugly and make him very sad and very angry. Not cross, you know, at having to write them down, because he is the Recording Angel and has got his duty to do and doesn't expect it always to be easy and pleasant. But he is sad and angry too, just as we are and have a right to be, when he has to record all the treacherous and cruel things thought out and taught and practised by people who meant to make war for their own profit and didn't mean even then to fight fair. And there are a lot of other ugly things he has to put down in his book, about people who had always been greedy about money and thought the war was just an extra fine chance of making more money for themselves, —though as they grow richer they grow greedier too, so that even the money they gain is no good to them; and people who found cosy corners for themselves at home, when they were wanted, and were young and strong enough, to go and serve abroad; and people who were selfish enough to go on strike at times and refuse to dig out coal or to make shells or ships or aeroplanes until some little grievance was put right, and never bothered to remember that the men who were fighting for them had lots of grievances too, real sufferings and hardships all day and all night, not just petty little things to grumble at, and that they went on fighting just the same. All those things look very ugly to Uriel, because when a country is fighting against a cruel and treacherous enemy it is so simple for people to know what they ought to do. They can help or they can hinder; and if a man helps to his utmost, he is doing his duty to his country and her good cause; and when he hinders or doesn't help, he is false to both and, for what he is worth, a traitor.

But there are a lot of lovely things too in Uriel's big book. On some pages, before the war began, there were a lot of bad marks, far more bad ones than good; and Uriel could see that the people whose names were written at the top of those pages were getting more idle and selfish and really bad each year; and, though their guardian-angels whispered to them sometimes what was happening to them, they didn't seem to wake up or care. And then the war came and they woke up and saw just one thing clear, their duty to go and fight for their country, which deep down in their hearts they had always loved better than themselves; and their guardian-angels sent messages to Uriel that they had really turned over a new leaf. So Uriel turned over a new leaf in his big book too, and on the new page there are hardly any bad marks,—perhaps just a few in the column headed "Words," because a lot of soldiers and sailors do use naughty words; even captains of ships and colonels haven't always learnt better; but they don't often mean any harm by them.

Of course the records under a lot of names are very short, and it makes Uriel sad in a way that all those lives should have ended so soon. It is not so much that he is sorry for the men who have died; he knows they are happy, still watching and helping those whom they love; but he is very sorry for all the mothers and wives and children who miss them, and he sometimes thinks too, half wistfully, of all the other beautiful things he would have had to write about them in his book if they had lived longer. Not that he really minds, because he knows that the new work which they have been given is what God wanted them for even more; and when he makes the last entry about each of their lives in this world,—just the three words "Faithful unto death,"—he can't feel altogether sad. He has written them thousands and thousands of times lately, and if he wanted to save time he ought to have had a stamp; but he loves writing them with his own hand.

And it is not only about the men who have been fighting in the field or guarding the seas that Uriel has beautiful things to write. There are all the war-workers at home or abroad who have been serving where they were most wanted, or waiting patiently and cheerfully for the war to end and helping when they could,—women, and children too, as well as men. And most of the women I mean are not very much like the ladies with pretty dresses and smooth white hands whose photographs you may have seen in the picture-papers with "A Devoted War-worker" printed underneath. The ones I am thinking of have often got worn and roughened hands, and haven't bought themselves lately any frocks they would care to be photographed in. They are in the hospitals, some of them, scrubbing and cooking as well as nursing; and in noisy factories making the same little piece of a shell or of a machine all day long; and stacking and labelling great bundles of clothes and boots in dreary warehouses; and trudging out in the mud on cold winter-mornings to their round of farm-work; and others again staying at home because there are children to be looked after, and working hard to save a little money here and there so that the children may have food and warmth and clothing. And the children themselves too, when they just laugh over having to do without the nice things and the treats they used to have, and when they run errands to save tired people trouble, and plan surprises to make the beds, and lay the table, and wash up afterwards, all by themselves,—Uriel has a very gentle smile when he makes notes about them too.

But all the same a big book like that naturally doesn't interest the elves much, because they don't know the people whose names are there and haven't much to do with men and women or even children; their people are the animals and birds and insects and flowers. Besides they don't have or want books—not even picture-books or scrap-books—for themselves; so of course they wouldn't care much about Uriel's monstrous great ledger.

I needn't tell you about the guardian-angels. You know how everybody has one to look after him, chiefly by putting good thoughts into his mind and gently reminding him of what the people at home who love him would like him to do and how he can best help God, but also by guarding him from dangers and soothing his sufferings until the day comes when

God wants him for some other work. But it isn't men only who have guardian-angels; there are a sort of guardian-angels to look after the animals too, and they are called warden-elves. "Warden" really means just the same as "guardian," only we don't use it so often. Some schools and colleges have a man called the Warden in charge of them, and of course there are church-wardens too; and they have to look after the school or college or church just like the warden-elves look after the birds and beasts and flowers. Apart from that the elves aren't very like wardens of colleges or church-wardens, who nearly always wear black coats and are often stout and even wheezy. But then there are people called guardians too who have meetings to talk about workhouses, and how much money is to be spent on the poor people in them, and some of them think more about saving money than about the poor people they are supposed to look after; so these aren't very like guardian-angels either, except just in name.

I don't suppose that there is one warden-elf for each animal in the same way that there is one guardian-angel for each person. A guardian-angel, I expect, often finds one man or woman or even one child quite a handful; but an elf wouldn't have enough to do very often in looking after one animal only. It might be a caterpillar which doesn't do much but browse at any time, and ends by spinning a cocoon or burrowing in the ground and turning into a chrysalis; and you wouldn't expect an elf just to sit down and watch the chrysalis all the winter and wait for a butterfly to come out. Or it might be a dormouse which doesn't like cold weather, and so when the summer ends makes himself a warm cosy nest in a hedge and goes to sleep till he can feel the sunshine again; so if he had a warden-elf all to himself, there would be a long idle time for the elf each winter. What I expect the elves do is to divide up all the country and look after all the animals in their own little wards,—some of them up on the mountains, and some in the woodlands, and others in the meadows and along the streams where so many animals come to drink.

But of course some of the elves must be free to go away from their wards. A lot of the birds, you know, migrate to some warmer country a long, long way off at the end of every summer and come back to us in the spring; there wouldn't be shelter or food for them here all the winter when the trees are stripped bare and everything may be covered with snow for days on end. You must have seen the swallows collected in flocks,—along the telegraph-wires very often,—all ready to start; and lots of other birds make up big parties in the same way and fly off together thousands of miles. All the trains in the world don't carry as many passengers at once as there

2—2

are birds migrating. It is lucky they have no luggage because even without any they keep the elves very busy.

Some of the elves have to go with each flock of birds, to show them the way and to tell them where there are stopping-places with plenty of the right sort of berries or other food, and water too; and ready, some of them, to stay behind with any stragglers who get tired and can't keep up, and to bring them along later, perhaps with another party. You can fancy what a lot of arranging it all wants when there are thousands and thousands of birds all flying thousands and thousands of miles twice in the year, going away in the autumn and coming back in the spring. And what's more, a good many of them like to come back to their old homes and make their nests in exactly the same tree as the year before; so there must be a lot of elves looking after them to see that they all get to the right places.

And then when the birds come home in the spring the elves' work isn't finished. There are so many of the birds who have never made a nest yet or seen other birds making one; and it has got to be done so carefully. It is quite a different matter from what animals like rabbits have to do. Little rabbits have seen their fathers and mothers scratching new burrows lots of times, and have tried doing it themselves for fun; and so, when they grow up and want a home of their own, they know all about burrowing already and they can easily choose for themselves how many rooms they want, and where they will have the parlour and the nursery and the bedrooms; it is just a matter of scratching with their paws. But the birds have a lot to learn before they can make their first nests. They may just remember the sort of place they lived in when they were quite small,—that it was a snug hole in a branch or in a bank, or a sort of mossy ball in a bush with a curtain of leaves all round, or a great bundle of sticks and grasses high up on some bough that swayed when the wind blew, or a funny cup of clay, on a rafter or under the eaves of a roof, not very pretty outside but beautifully warm and cosy inside even if it was raining. But of course they can't remember how those nests were made; when they came out of their shells they found themselves inside a nest, and it wasn't until they began to fly that they could even see what the outside of it looked like, and they don't know a bit how it was built.

So the elves have to teach them about the different kinds of stuff that are wanted for each kind of nest, and how to bend and reeve and make fast. There are sticks and straws, and dry leaves and grasses, and moss and wool and horse-hair and feathers; and first the coarser and stronger bits have to be laid well and truly like the keel of a ship, so that the whole nest won't topple over; and then the sides have to be woven together piece by piece firmly and soundly so as to keep the wind and rain out; and the lining very often has to be something very soft and warm and cosy, because the little birds when they come out of the eggs haven't got any feathers to speak of.

And then there are the different shapes of nests to think about. Some of the big birds have a fairly flat platform of sticks so that their little ones can learn to stand steady on their legs and practise flapping their wings a little before they try to fly; and water-birds, like moorhens, mostly have flat nests too, sometimes in a tuft of rushes only just above the water, so that their chicks can slip quietly into the water without taking a header, and can climb into the nest again easily when they are tired of swimming. But most birds like a nice deep cup-shaped nest because it isn't so draughty for the quite little birds; and it keeps them from tumbling out too when they get a little bigger and scramble for the bits of food the father and mother birds bring them. And then there are just a few birds, like wrens, who want a roof over their nests and a little round window to fly in and out of in one side. And there are others who are ready to take a lot of trouble to prevent their nests showing, —like chaffinches, who often build in the fork of an apple-tree and pick little bits of dried moss and lichen off the trunks of other apple-trees and dot them over the outside of their nests to make them look like part of the boughs on which they rest. That is what the soldiers have been doing too with their big guns in this war,—what they call "camouflage,"— painting the guns or covering them with branches and things so that they look from a distance like part of the ground where they stand. But the elves had been teaching the birds how to camouflage their nests long before soldiers ever thought of it.

So you see what busy little folk the elves must be with all the animals and birds to look after.

But isn't it a lovely surprise they planned for their big brother Michael, that when he came home he should find that they were helping to look after men too, his own comrades? I wonder what made them think of it. Perhaps it was the rabbits and moles who came and said to them "Where are we to live now? The men who used to live in houses have all taken to burrowing, and as soon as they have made their burrows other men throw big things at them which go bang and spoil them; and it isn't safe for us any- where." Or perhaps it was a squirrel who had picked a lot of nuts and put them in a hole in some tree which he used as his storeroom, and one day, when he was hungry and went to get some out, found, not just the branch, where the hole was, blown down by the wind—some elf would soon have found his larder for him again, if that had been all—but something much worse, the whole tree knocked to splinters and his nuts gone for good. And when it went on and on like that, the elves began to wonder what had happened to make men who had a guardian-angel each to look after them fight worse than the wild animals ever do.

Of course they don't like the animals fighting; they wish that foxes would learn to feed on grass like rabbits and not go killing other animals, and that hawks would leave field-mice and little birds alone and live on berries instead. Still they know that that is just the hawks' and foxes' nature and can't be helped. And even men, they see, are no better than foxes in that, and have to kill animals for food. The elves themselves don't need any food except the scent of flowers, violets and thyme and rosemary and meadowsweet, but they know that men and animals want something much more filling. It did puzzle them, though, why men everywhere should suddenly begin fighting—for no reason that the elves knew of, because they had never had much to do with men and had rather kept away from the houses where they lived and the roads along which they walked or drove.

And perhaps in the end they asked Gabriel why men seemed suddenly to have gone wild instead of living at home in peace. And he would have told them that most of the men who were fighting didn't like wars any more than Michael did, but they knew too like Michael when to fight and how to fight; and so when the people of one big country broke all their promises and began robbing and killing the people of a little peaceful country, the men of other countries, however much they loved peace, had to join in the fight, to succour the weak and to punish the wicked. And for that they had to be very pitiful and very stern as well; pitiful above all for the women and children they were trying to guard and save, just as all the angels and elves are pitiful in guarding and saving the men or the animals they look after; and stern as Michael was when once there was war in heaven.

And then I expect the elves asked Gabriel if they could do anything to help the men who were fighting so bravely for the sake of others, or the women and children that those men were trying to keep safe. And Gabriel said that there wasn't really anything the elves could do to help the men who were still fighting in the field. They were much too little to go and fight beside them like Michael and his soldier-angels; and Raphael had plenty of trained seraphim to help in looking after the wounded; and there was a guardian-angel too with each man night and day, so that there was nothing that could hurt or touch him so long as God wanted him in the trenches. And naturally when God sent orders that a man's work in the firing-line was finished and that he had been promoted and attached to the real G.H.Q. for duties on God's personal staff, there would be still less room for the elves to help in any way. Still there was one thing they might do for the men who had been called away, and it would be a comfort too to the women and children left behind. And then perhaps he told them a little about the women and the children at home, and how brave they had been at each parting, and how they had hoped and prayed that God would spare them that long last parting; and how before, when it was only the sea that parted them, they had been able to send and to get letters, and to knit warm socks and scarves which their men would wear. And then suddenly for many and many of them the long last parting had come, and it was no good going on with the socks they were knitting, because their men wear another uniform now—the elves would see them perhaps on All Souls' Day, a multitude that none can number, clothed in white raiment; and the women couldn't even go and lay flowers on their graves. So there was that one thing the elves could do for those brave men, which would comfort the women and children too. They could plant flowers on those graves, and that would give their little hands work for many a long day.

And I'm sure that Gabriel must have told them too that it was not only their hands which could help, but their lips and hearts as well. They could join with angels and archangels and all the company of saints on earth and saints in heaven in praying God to give peace and to hasten the time when He should wipe away tears from all eyes.

And so it came about that some of the elves set to work to plant flowers on all those graves, choosing pansies and forget-me-nots as their song tells you. Forget-me-nots of course, but do you know why they chose the little wild pansies too? Because pansy is really a French word *pensée* which means "thought" or "remembrance," and so the meaning of those two flowers is that those graves will never be forgotten in England or in France. And perhaps too they planted the pansies in the middle and the forget-me-nots round outside because the ground of France has been the middle point of the war and England's arms have enfolded her as the seas enfold the land.

And as the elves went about their task of tending the graves day by day and saw acre upon acre of holy ground stretching in a broad band from Flanders to the borders of Switzerland, or dotted over all the Eastern lands to which the great crusade had spread, they remembered perhaps and understood better what Gabriel had said about the multitude that none can number whom they might see on All Souls' Day; and they may have begun to wonder who would make all the white raiment for that multitude of brave souls to wear, now that their mothers and wives and children couldn't send them parcels any more. And then too there would be a lot of handkerchiefs wanted if they were going to ask God to hasten the time for wiping away tears from all eyes. If they could go where the women couldn't, and plant flowers on the graves, why shouldn't they do some needlework too instead of the mothers and wives and children who couldn't send theirs any longer?

And so some more elves, who were still busy in the woods and fields looking after the animals, set to work to gather gossamer. Do you know what gossamer is? It is a fine, soft, glistening thread, like spiders' webs sparkling with the dew at daybreak; but whether it is real gossamer or fairy gossamer which the elves use, and how they dye it for their embroidery, I can't tell you. Perhaps it is just the gossamer of the hedgerows gathered by the elves and spun by them into silken threads; and if they want to dye the threads, they hang them among the tall grasses or the corn where the flowers grow brightest, and the butterflies that hover from flower to flower powder them with the painted dust of their wings. Or maybe it is fairy gossamer spun from wisps of fleecy cloud and dipped by some elfin magic in the blue and silver of a moonlit sea, or the purple shadows of the mountains, or the green and gold and crimson of the sunset.

And all the time, while they were planting, or spinning and weaving and embroidering, their hearts were as full of prayer as their hands were of flowers or gossamer, and the prayer was not for themselves but always for those for whom they were working, that God would give peace; and out of the fullness of their hearts their lips could sing no song that was not a prayer for peace; and new words set themselves to the old tunes and always with the refrain "Give peace, dear God," till even in the singing of the birds and the whispering of the forest-trees, and in the burbling of the streams and the lapping of the waves, they seemed to hear the same refrain, "Give peace, dear God," and it reminded them of the litanies of the angels. And then they thought perhaps how lovely it would be to have a litany of the elves as well, and how pleased Michael would be with their surprise when he came home and heard them sing it; and it would be lovelier still when he saw how they had taught the wild creatures of the woods and hills and rivers, just as they themselves had been taught by Gabriel, to join with the angels and archangels and all the company of Michael's comrades in one song of prayer.

And so the litany of the elves, when All Saints' Day and All Souls' Day came, seemed to them like a cry from the heart of all creation.

And very soon God gave peace.

www.ingramcontent.com/pod-product-compliance
Ingram Content Group UK Ltd.
Pitfield, Milton Keynes, MK11 3LW, UK
UKHW042156280225
455719UK00001B/369